D0145395

POCKET STUDY SKILLS

Series Editor: **Kate Williams**, *Oxford Brookes University, UK*
Illustrations by Sallie Godwin

For the time-pushed student, the *Pocket Study Skills* pack a lot of advice into a little book. Each guide focuses on a single crucial aspect of study giving you step-by-step guidance, handy tips and clear advice on how to approach the important areas which will continually be at the core of your studies.

Published

Pocket Study Skills
Series Standing Order
ISBN 978–0230–21605–1
(outside North America only)

You can receive future titles in this series as they are published by placing a standing order. Please contact your bookseller or, in case of difficulty, write to us at the address below with your name and address, the title of the series and the ISBN quoted above.

Customer Services Department, Macmillan Distribution Ltd, Houndmills, Basingstoke, Hampshire RG21 6XS England

STUDYING WITH DYSLEXIA

POCKET STUDY SKILLS

Janet Godwin

palgrave
macmillan

© Janet Godwin 2012

All rights reserved. No reproduction, copy or transmission of this publication may be made without written permission.

No portion of this publication may be reproduced, copied or transmitted save with written permission or in accordance with the provisions of the Copyright, Designs and Patents Act 1988, or under the terms of any licence permitting limited copying issued by the Copyright Licensing Agency, Saffron House, 6-10 Kirby Street, London EC1N 8TS.

Any person who does any unauthorized act in relation to this publication may be liable to criminal prosecution and civil claims for damages. The author has asserted her right to be identified as the author of this work in accordance with the Copyright, Designs and Patents Act 1988.

First published 2012 by
PALGRAVE MACMILLAN

Palgrave Macmillan in the UK is an imprint of Macmillan Publishers Limited, registered in England, company number 785998, of Houndmills, Basingstoke, Hampshire RG21 6XS.

Palgrave Macmillan in the US is a division of St Martin's Press LLC, 175 Fifth Avenue, New York, NY 10010.

Palgrave Macmillan is the global academic imprint of the above companies and has companies and representatives throughout the world.

Palgrave® and Macmillan® are registered trademarks in the United States, the United Kingdom, Europe and other countries

ISBN: 978–0–230–39056–0

This book is printed on paper suitable for recycling and made from fully managed and sustained forest sources. Logging, pulping and manufacturing processes are expected to conform to the environmental regulations of the country of origin.

A catalogue record for this book is available from the British Library.

A catalog record for this book is available from the Library of Congress.

10 9 8 7 6 5 4 3 2 1
21 20 19 18 17 16 15 14 13 12

Printed and bound in China

Contents

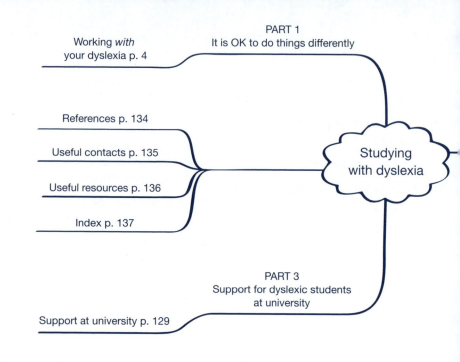

Contents

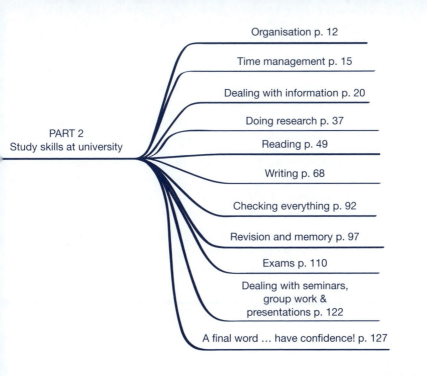

Acknowledgements

My thanks go to my students, who have taught me everything I know about how to support them. I never cease to be inspired by both their determination and the effort made to achieve academically, despite their SpLD (Specific Learning Difference). Particular thanks go to those who allowed me to use them as an example for this book.

Thanks also to Kate Williams for her patience and support in the writing of this little book and to colleagues who agreed to be my 'critical friends' for their supportive comments and sensible suggestions. Finally, a special thanks to my daughter Sallie for her witty and perceptive illustrations which enliven the series.

The author and publishers also wish to thank the following for permission to reproduce copyright material: Sonocent, Houghton Mifflin Company, R. David Middlebrook, University of Hull, Mercier Press and Westminster School.

Introduction

It takes enormous effort for dyslexic students to keep up with their studies at university. Most know dyslexia involves memory problems but do not take up the one-to-one support they may be entitled to. As a dyslexic student you may not realise that understanding your dyslexia means YOU can manage your dyslexia positively and so work with it, not against it.

This little book is about understanding there is a dyslexic learning style and using this to think about how to tackle a task before starting it. This will reduce your workload and increase your efficiency. It should also reduce the stress so many dyslexic students experience and the impact of dyslexia on your studies.

Strategies are suggested throughout the book to work with the dyslexic learning style. It is hoped you will try these out and use any you find useful. Please discard any that don't work for you. After reading this book you should be able to consider what else you could use that would fit in with your dyslexic learning style.

It is all about finding out what works for you and doing it your way!

How to use this guide

This guide does not need to be read all at once. Just keep coming back to it for ideas from time to time.

Part 1 explains why dyslexia makes studying harder and gives ideas about how to work *with* your dyslexia and not against it. This puts YOU in charge of your dyslexia, not the other way round.

Part 2 concentrates on individual skills such as reading, writing and dealing with information. These can be read in any order – just dip in and out as needed.

Part 3 provides some information on what support should be available to you at university. It is worth looking at this if you are (or suspect you are) dyslexic.

IT IS OK TO DO THINGS DIFFERENTLY

Learn to work *with* your dyslexia

The main message of this book is that IT IS OK to do things differently. You may have tried working in the same way as your friends – maybe taking notes in a lecture or working at the last minute through the night only to find that you don't understand what you have written. It is likely that these methods just don't seem to work for you. Give yourself permission to explore ways of working that will use your dyslexia constructively.

Being dyslexic does not mean you are not as bright as other people – just that you learn differently. You can be clever and dyslexic; dyslexia does not determine your intelligence.

Some famous people are dyslexic: Steve Redgrave, Kara Tointon, Eddie Izzard, Jamie Oliver, Keira Knightley, Stephen Spielberg, Kirstie Allsopp, Cher and even Walt Disney.

It is reckoned that 10% of students are dyslexic, so you are in good company.

Characteristics of dyslexia

What is dyslexia? A simple question, but one there has been much debate about. It is not important for you to understand everything about dyslexia, and every dyslexic person is unique, but you will share some characteristics.

Characteristics of dyslexia include:

▶ short-term memory (or working memory) is not as efficient as that of non-dyslexics
▶ speed of processing information is slower than for non-dyslexics.

The good news is that your long-term memory is likely to be very good: once you have learnt something you really get it.

Why this matters

Simply put, it takes you much longer to process and remember information. This is why you are allowed extra time in exams and why it takes you ages to research and write your assignments.

These memory and processing difficulties mean your phonological knowledge (knowing how groups of letters represent sounds and the ability to put these together accurately) is not as developed as that of other learners. Reading and writing is not automatic or fluent for you. Comprehension of text is affected and spelling may also be erratic.

The same difficulties that affect reading and writing also affect organisation skills. These include managing time, organising ideas and structuring assignments.

Understanding short-term (working) memory – and why it matters!

It is necessary to learn a little more about **short-term (or working memory)** and **speed of processing information** to understand how you can learn effectively.

Why this matters

It takes much more effort for dyslexics to learn NEW information. The only sure way is to **over-learn** material by going over and over it until you know it perfectly. All students learn this way, but it is much more important for dyslexic students, who cannot rely on learning quickly or at the last minute.

OVER-LEARNING means reviewing your work OFTEN

Understanding Information processing – and why it matters!

You probably knew your short-term memory is not as good as your friends'. The other characteristic of dyslexia – slow information processing speed – may be new to you.

Speed of information processing

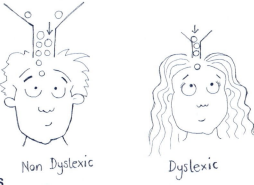

Non Dyslexic   Dyslexic

Why this matters

Just when you need to deal with lots of information – say in a lecture – your speed of processing clogs up. This makes it almost impossible to listen *and* take notes, or, when you are reading, comprehend *and* remember information.

Try to process a LITTLE information at a time

Work *with* your short-term memory by reviewing your stuff OFTEN – this is called over-learning. Avoid information overload by limiting how much information you process: work for short bursts of time. Then you process a LITTLE at a time.

Drip-feed knowledge a LITTLE at a time and do this OFTEN!

Think of this like filling a glass. We can either:

slowly fill the glass by dripping water in

Or we can:

fill it too fast and find some of it splashing back out again

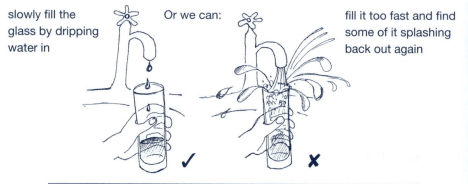

LITTLE and OFTEN – an effective dyslexic learning style
Over-learning and working for short periods of time works best

Working out your personal learning style

Your **personal learning style** is a combination of:

Dyslexic learning style Little and often	**+**	*Individual learning style* Visual – seeing Auditory – hearing/listening Kinaesthetic – doing

Knowing **which type of learner** you are allows you to adapt how you learn. If you are an auditory (verbal) learner, for example, using coloured mind maps may be a waste of time. If you learn by listening it would be better to discuss your work with a friend, or listen to recordings of notes, or use 'text-to-speech software' to have an article read to you.

If you do not know your individual learning style, try googling VAK (which stands for 'Visual, Auditory and Kinaesthetic'). You should soon find a questionnaire to do online.

Use your personal learning style and find out what works best for YOU.

Metacognition – or thinking about thinking

Metacognition means thinking about the processes involved when learning so that you understand how you learn best. This allows you to take control of organising your learning, monitoring your progress and achieving goals (Rose 2009).

Research (Torgesen 1981) shows that dyslexics find it hard to work out what a task involves and the best way to tackle it. Each new task is seen as a new problem and strategies already learned are not always applied.

This book is based on metacognition. It is about understanding how you learn and using strategies to become more effective in your work.

The aim is to end up with a reduced workload – which should also reduce stress. This is a bonus as the impact of dyslexia is usually worse when you are under stress.

STUDY SKILLS AT UNIVERSITY

Skills needed at university

University is different from your previous learning experiences and you need to develop particular skills to help you study independently.

This section shows how you can improve these skills by using both your personal learning style (visual, auditory or kinaesthetic) AND your dyslexic learning style (LITTLE and OFTEN).

organisation

note taking

writing

exams

research

time management

groupwork

reading

lectures & seminars

presentations

dealing with information

Using assistive technology (AT) to help

Assistive technology can help with organisation, reading, note taking, planning, researching, writing and checking work.

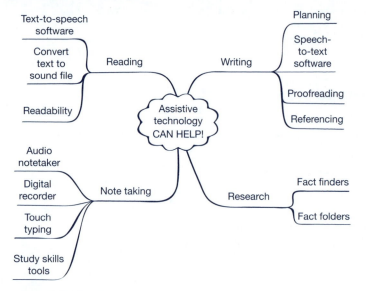

Students receiving DSA (Disabled Students' Allowance) funding usually get a computer with assistive software. This usually includes mind mapping software and text-to-speech software.

Most students do not realise how useful assistive technology is. The DSA pays for training to use the software – so make sure you use it! Training videos are usually available with the software and on the suppliers' web pages. Do browse through these so you can learn how the software can help you.

Some universities have site licences for assistive technology – useful if you are not eligible for DSA funding.

Also look for:

▸ free software, such as MyStudyBar available at: http://eduapps.org/?page_id=7

▸ free (limited day) downloads from some software suppliers.

See www.yourdsa.com for a list of suppliers and links to free stuff

2 Organisation

The characteristics of dyslexia (slow information processing speed and short-term memory) ALSO cause problems with **organisation.**

This includes many types of organisation: juggling time, work, family and social life, daily living tasks, academic tasks, and even structuring assignments.

As you cannot rely on your memory, some sort of organising tool is a must. Take your pick from the table below. Use one from each time zone:

Time zone	Consider using	Comments
Semester	Semester planner, wall planner, mobile phone	Take note of coursework type (essay, presentation), day due, % worth of total marks
Week	Online calendar, diary, timetable, 'to do' list	Colour code different activities so you can see them at a glance
Day	'To do' list, diary, calendar, timetable, Stickies/Post-it® notes	These can be on computer, a notebook, mobile or anything

It does not matter what you use ... just don't rely on your wobbly memory!

Extensions: DON'T! unless the situation looks completely lost. You will only pay for it later – and have less time for other coursework or exam revision.

Organisation: how will you deal with the paperwork?

Not everything can be stored on the computer, so you need a system to deal with all the paper you collect. Do this before you have other things to worry about – exams, for instance.

Make sure you have files and dividers and consider doing these:

Files:

▶ Colour code course files – a different colour for each study unit.
▶ Keep course files in your room and have one file that you take into uni/college (use dividers for different units). Every week or so, review and file your notes in the course files.

- Use a separate file or box file for each piece of coursework so you can keep all the resources for it together.

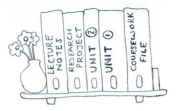

Notes:

Lecture notes: Write course name/code, date and number on *every* page.

From reading: Record as much of the reference as you can.

Pick a time once a week when you review, check and file paperwork, set your alarm in your mobile!

3 Time management

You will have noticed it takes you longer to do tasks than other students. In a seminar or lecture you may not be able to finish reading something in the time allowed. When studying alone you may not be aware just how much time you are taking over some activities. There is a big difference in the time you *estimate* a task will take and the *actual* time you spent doing it.

Help yourself by noticing where the time goes.

1 Think of a task you have done recently – maybe reading a chapter of a book or reviewing your notes.
2 Note down the total time it took to do (**actual** time).
3 How much time did you think it would take? (**estimated** time).
4 Putting it in a table may help you see which activities take most time.

Task	Estimated time (ET)	Actual time (AT)
Breakfast	10 mins	All morning …
Reading – Chap. 2 sociology book	2 hours	5 hours
Reviewing notes for week 1	Half hour	3 hours
Your example?		

This exercise helps identify which activities take more time than you realised.

Aim to use the **estimated** time only, and adapt how you do the task to fit this. For instance: use the start/end reading method (pp. 58–62) for the **estimated time only**, then stop. Or when reviewing notes spend a minute or two per page only (see the Cornell note-taking system pp. 34–6) or use Stickies/Post-it notes to summarise.

Notice when you work best

Spend a few minutes now considering when you are at your best to work. This could save you hours of wasted effort.

These are Oli's best and worst working times:

Early morning	Morning	Lunchtime	Early afternoon	Late afternoon	Evening	Late evening
No way!	?	Yes	No	Yes	No	Yes

What are yours? Fill in the table:

Early morning	Morning	Lunchtime	Early afternoon	Late afternoon	Evening	Late evening

Tasks to do when alert	Tasks to do when less alert
Reading, searching databases, taking notes from reading

Add your thoughts here: | Shopping, organising notes, finding books, eating, going for a walk, reviewing last week's notes, starting a reference list

Add your thoughts here: |

How long can you work effectively for?

How long is it before you get distracted when working? 10 minutes? 20 minutes? Less? More? This will, of course, depend on the activity you are doing.

Dyslexia means you quickly become overloaded with information. Your brain tries to protect you by daydreaming or even dozing off. It is best to STOP before this happens, if you can.

Learn to recognise when you are working effectively (and when you are not). STOP as soon as you are getting distracted as this indicates you are becoming overloaded. Take a short break (or change to a lighter activity).

Vicky, a Social Care student, said:

'I can't believe how my 10-minute rule has changed everything. I even stop my friends going on by putting my hand up and saying, "Sorry 10 mins up – I am not receiving!"'

Vicky realised she concentrates quite well for up to 10 minutes. Then her attention drifts off. Now Vicky notices when this happens and cuts short any activities (even conversations!). This means she is working *with* her dyslexia, not against it. She is being effective by recognising when she is being ineffective.

Working for lots of short periods of time is much better than sitting down for 2 hours but only actually working effectively for 20 minutes of this. The graphs below illustrate how building in lots of breaks really will increase your effectiveness.

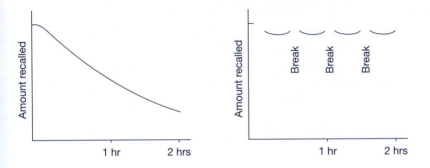

Dyslexia and dealing with information

Dealing with information is your biggest challenge as a dyslexic student at university or college. Most dyslexic students are aware that they work much harder than their non-dyslexic friends and are not always rewarded with the grades they think they deserve. Dyslexia affects how well you can process information, and your short-term memory means it takes time to learn effectively. Given time, you can deal with information effectively.

You have a choice:

either

you can just carry on trying to do everything, which will result in you becoming increasingly exhausted as the year continues …

or

you can take steps to reduce your workload and become more efficient.

Applying the dyslexic learning style (LITTLE and OFTEN) whenever possible will help. Consider your personal learning style (visual, auditory or kinaesthetic) when choosing a strategy to cope with the information you will have to deal with.

How to start reducing your workload

Previously, you have been directed to the information needed for your courses and provided with notes, handouts and the required reading. University is different. Lectures and seminars provide the main ideas and themes to consider, but then it is up to you to find out more for yourself.

You'll have to learn the best way for YOU to process the information from:

Lectures

    Seminars

        Reading lists

            Research

                Course information

                    VLE (virtual learning environment)

It is easy to become overwhelmed by the sheer volume of information. However, you can help yourself a lot if you begin by considering *why* you have been set a task – your tutor will have had a *purpose* in mind. Then you need to choose a way to tackle the task that fits with this purpose.

Task	Purpose	Why	Which means ...	Strategy
1 Pre-reading for lecture	Prepare for lecture	Pick up main ideas – fast	Don't need detailed reading	Read the abstract, the introduction and conclusion, then headings/subheadings
2 Revision of subject	Fill in the gaps	Complete knowledge	Only do bits you don't know	List the areas not yet tackled. Do in order of importance.
Your example here?				

1 Reading *all* the suggested pre-reading in detail would take ages. However, if you choose to apply the 'start and end' method of reading (pp. 58–62), you will get the main ideas without deep reading the whole chapter or article. By fitting what you did to the purpose you have reduced your workload.

2 Revising only the bits you have not covered before (filling in the gaps) helps target your revision so that you don't waste time on things you already know well.

This is using metacognition to think about the PURPOSE first and then using this to pick a suitable STRATEGY – so you only do the work **actually needed.**

Making informed choices like this puts YOU in charge – and increases your efficiency.

> Before starting a task, consider what the PURPOSE is and WHY it was set

Virtual learning environment

Your university will have a virtual learning environment (VLE). This is a web-based resource that can be accessed when you are off-site. Do go hunting around it: your tutors will assume you have looked at any material they put on the VLE.

Advantages

All your course information will be there, such as handbooks and PowerPoint slides of notes

You cannot lose it!

It may have other resources your tutors think are useful.

Your one-to-one specialist support tutor can see any course guidance you have

But you may:

– not know what is on it

– dislike working on the PC

– lack confidence in your IT skills

– not get around to reading it (although tutors will assume you have!)

> VLEs are an invaluable resource. Make sure you can access and use yours

Your course handbook

This is essential reading! It should tell you:

Learning outcomes
(what you need to show
in your work)

Assessment criteria
(what they want!)

Reading lists

**Coursework/exam
information**

Suggestions for **how to
tackle assignment**(s)

Lectures at university

Lectures are the main point of contact between teaching staff and students at university. They provide a foundation or starting point for your studies.

So you can expect to study independently for many hours outside the time spent in lectures.

A course unit may have:

150 hours total study time – but only *30 hours* contact time

So *120 hours* are independent study time.

You will have three or four separate courses, so this is a lot of individual study!

Practical or scientific subjects require more contact time in university as you will also have practical or laboratory sessions. Arts subjects such as History or English may have very little time spent in lectures or seminars.

Knowing this can help you put lectures in perspective: their main PURPOSE is to open up the possibilities or main ideas associated with that subject … not provide everything you need to know.

Attendance is important as you'll find out you what you should focus on, but it may not be necessary for you to record everything the lecturer says.

At university lectures are the just starting point for your studies

Note taking in lectures

Ask yourself this question: *What do I do with my lecture notes?*

Answer the question honestly; it makes a difference to how you deal with note taking in lectures.

Consider not taking notes!

Most dyslexic students try hard to take notes in lectures but find they can either follow what is being said OR take notes. Not BOTH!

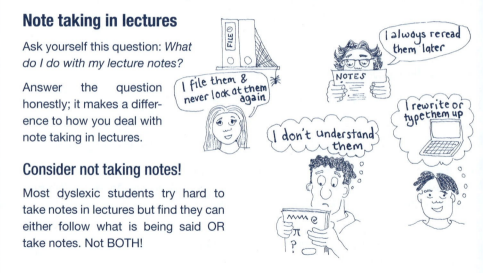

If this is you:

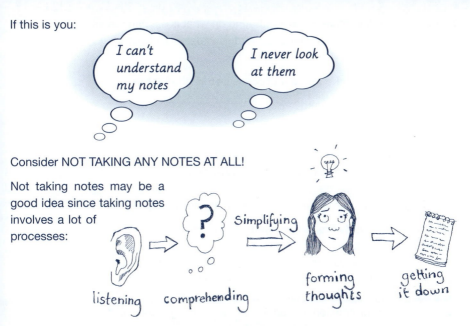

Consider NOT TAKING ANY NOTES AT ALL!

Not taking notes may be a good idea since taking notes involves a lot of processes:

Doing all this requires quick processing and good memory skills. These are not dyslexic strengths so note taking in lectures works against your dyslexic learning style.

You may understand more by concentrating on what is said and restricting any notes taken to main ideas, names of theorists and any references given so you can look them up later.

If you decide not to take notes, consider, before the lecture:

▶ **How will you keep focused?**

Suggestions include:

- ▶ recording the lecture
- ▶ using audio notetaker software (see p. 33)
- ▶ ticking off where you are on any notes provided
- ▶ doodling (can help you focus on what is being said)
- ▶ creating diagrams, mind maps, keywords for any resources mentioned.

▶ **How will you review the lecture material?**

Suggestions include:

- ▶ immediately afterwards writing down everything you can recall
- ▶ going for coffee with a friend and discussing the lecture
- ▶ finding suggested reading (see course information)
- ▶ following up information on handouts – and adding in new notes
- ▶ asking your subject librarian to help find sources.

Unhelpful strategies you may have to change

In your previous learning you were probably given lots of notes and didn't really need to do much research outside this. University is different because you have to develop knowledge and understanding beyond your lecture materials.

Try to avoid doing the following; they are a waste of time and effort:

▶ **copying out notes** – it is not possible to keep up with the volume of rewriting and this will prevent you developing your knowledge *outside* that presented in the lecture.
▶ **worrying about neat notes** – the only requirement for your notes is that you understand them. They are a working document and do not need to be neat. They are for your eyes only.
▶ **trying to write down everything** – this will only result in notes you don't understand. Make as brief notes as you can. You may be given handouts, which you can add brief notes to.

You could change your strategy: If you are still doing any the above, think how you could adapt this and save time. Maybe you could record thoughts from your notes on a digital recorder or mind map or reduce these onto a sticky note. These are all quicker than rewriting.

Tips that work when you have to take notes

Avoid taking notes

Just note down where you can find the information later on, plus key information such as names of researchers and theories.

Preview any notes available

Do this *before* the lecture if possible. This works because it allows you to process more information in the actual lecture. Just knowing the format of the lecture in advance helps (you'll notice when the lecturer goes off track!).

Reduce amount of notes you take

Always ask the lecturer for notes. Even better – ask them to put them up on any e-learning environment your university has (and *before* the lecture if possible). Can you photocopy someone else's notes?

TIP 4

Use your learning style

Decide what method of note taking may work for you:

Visual learner	use mind mapping, highlighting, coloured pens
Auditory learner	record notes and listen again later
Kinaesthetic learner	type notes using a laptop, mind mapping

Note-taking systems – selecting what works for you

There are two basic note-taking systems:

Linear   or   mind mapping

Arrabella (Primary
Teacher Education)

You can choose whichever one you are more comfortable with – or mix and match. Not *all* dyslexics like mind mapping!

Other useful note-taking strategies

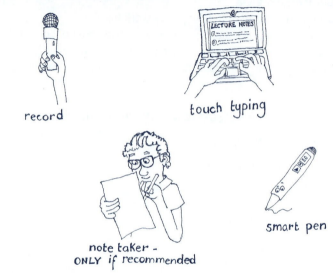

record

touch typing

note taker -
ONLY if recommended

smart pen

Smart pens can record lecture notes for replay. They usually require specialist note-paper (although a good-quality printer can reproduce usable notepaper).

Audio Notetaker is software for the PC and Mac which allows you to visualise your audio recordings and personalise them by adding colour, text, images and presentation slides. You can tag and organise your notes and also search for keywords. See www.sonocent.com

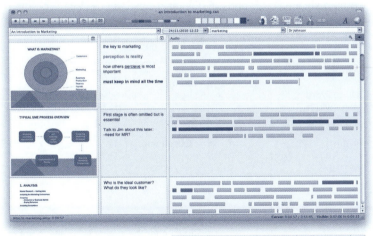

Image reproduced from www.sonocent.com/products/audio-notetaker/

The Cornell note-taking system (or two-column system)

If and when you have to take notes, select a note-taking system that works for you. Certainly try mind mapping or recording lectures … but there may be times when using a linear type system works. The Cornell note-taking system works well with the dyslexic learning style (LITTLE and OFTEN) as it has features that promote reviewing and revisiting your notes, which assists your learning process.

Divide an A4 sheet of paper as below. Use like this:

Review column	Notes
Up to 1/3rd of page width	Up to 2/3rd of page width
Summary 2" or about 7 lines	

Review column	Notes
Use for: Questions, Keywords Index	Take notes as usual, be brief, avoid sentences.
Summary Shortly after the lecture list, bullet point or mind map the most important points from your notes here.	

Method for Cornell note taking

During the lecture Record (brief) notes in the right-hand Notes column.

After the lecture Fill in the Summary box (after 24 hours or so). Note the main points. Be creative with colour, drawings, mini mind map, keywords or bullet points.

Later on ... Fill in the Review column – add questions, keywords, theory names, references, or build up an index so you can review your notes easily.

> Reviewing notes means you are actively working with them – and also memorising them!

The Cornell note-taking system – going deeper

The full version of the Cornell note-taking system suggests that you:

Record
    Question
        Recite
            Reflect
                Review
                    your notes.

Cornell note taking – going deeper

Record	Take notes using keywords/bullet points. Keep it brief!
Question	Write any questions you have in the Review column; this may be any gaps or anything you don't understand.
Recite	Look at questions and keywords. Say out loud what you can recall.
Reflect	Ask reflective questions: ▶ What's the significance of these facts? ▶ What principle are they based on? ▶ How can I apply them? ▶ How do they fit in with what I already know? ▶ What's beyond them?
Review	Spend time each week to browse through your notes. Focus on the Summary and Review column to start with.

Source: Adapted from *How to Study in College* (7th edition) by Walter Pauk (2001), Houghton Mifflin Company.

Here is a mind map to show how assistive technology can help with note taking:

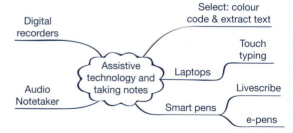

Before you rush off to collect resources …

It is a huge temptation to rush off to the library and collect as much information as you can. This is a mistake, especially if you are dyslexic.

You must **target** your research, or this might happen:

Your research (an elephant amount) won't fit into a matchbox ('word count')!

This is double (or even triple) trouble because you spent time finding the information, got confused as it *all* seemed so important, wrote it up, and finally spent hours cutting it down to fit your word count.

Word Count   Your Research

Here is a model of your course:

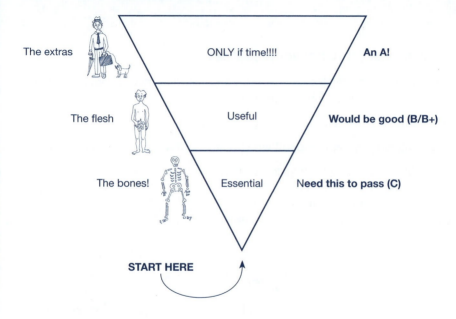

The extras   ONLY if time!!!!   **An A!**

The flesh   Useful   **Would be good (B/B+)**

The bones!   Essential   **Need this to pass (C)**

START HERE

To achieve a grade	You must ...
C – a pass	... cover the bottom triangle. This is the essential knowledge and understanding needed, or the bones of the course.
B – would be good	... include the important knowledge too – the bones fleshed out.
A – only if time	... add the extra details, like clothes and accessories – but only if you have time!

This fits in well with the dyslexic learning style of LITTLE and OFTEN, as each time you return to a subject you add a few more layers. You are doing the *over-learning process* that is essential to the dyslexic learning style.

Ideally this happens ...

You build up your knowledge and understanding from the essentials (a C) to the useful (a B) then – only if you have time – to an A with any extra detail.

$$C \longrightarrow B \longrightarrow A$$

Knowledge is built up a little at a time, working with your short-term memory and adding more detail each time – and working *with* your dyslexic learning style.

But the dyslexic tendency is to do this in reverse, so ...

... you try to do everything in the detail needed to get an A. This is hard enough without dyslexia, but add in the dyslexic difficulties of slow information processing speed and memory issues and you can see this is heading for trouble.

$$A \longrightarrow B \longrightarrow C$$

This explains why you may get variable grades. If you are lucky and your essay or exam matches with the bits you did in detail then you get the A. Usually, though, this is a bit hit-and-miss. If bits of the essential stuff were skipped you risk not doing so well. In extreme cases you may fail, despite knowing some of it to an A standard.

The key to this is **reducing your workload** so that you can confidently apply the dyslexic learning style of LITTLE and OFTEN to different learning situations.

Reduce your workload!

This is crucial to your success at university; you simply *must not* try to do everything. You need to think about how you tackle your learning – see metacognition (p. 8). This

is vital if you are dyslexic since it takes so much longer to research, read up, write and check assignments and revise for exams.

Starting university is rather like entering a race: you need to get to the finish line in the quickest time and go straight there, not wander around the track aimlessly or collapse long before you get there.

You could:

Try to do it all

OR

collect loads sort it later

OR

THINK how to tackle it

So

reducing how much you have to do

Doing it all is exhausting and not effective in the end

Try these strategies:

When	Try	If it goes wrong
Reading …	Ask 'what do I need to find out?' Write it down and only do this.	Note the reference of anything interesting; *briefly* note what it is. Now leave it alone! You have the reference if you need it for later.
Researching …	Ask yourself what you already know, then identify gaps. Target research carefully.	If you find yourself randomly researching then try to see where the new information will fit in. If you can't, leave that topic for now.
Writing …	Frame and fill (p. 76).	Map out a mini plan of what you could cover then ✓, ✗ or ? ideas. Only use ticked bits for now. You can 'fill in' later.
Revising …	Prioritise topics. Look at past papers; some topics always come up.	Too many areas to cover? Use Cornell method (pp. 34–6). For notes already taken use Stickies or Post-its to summarise. Start with the basics. Add detail later.

Reducing what you research by keeping things simple will help

Keep it simple – tips for dyslexics

Reduce the amount of information you have to deal with by recognising when you are overcomplicating your task, going off at a tangent or just doing too much detail. These are very dyslexic traits. Avoid unnecessary work:

▶ Start with the **basics** and **build** up to a full picture
▶ Recognise if you are an **over-researcher**
▶ Notice when you are '**mind wandering**'

Basics first Build up your understanding, bit by bit. Think of this as starting with the skeleton and gradually adding layers:

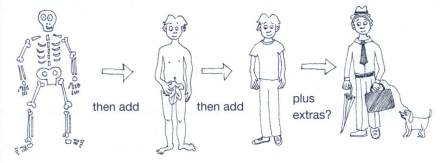

then add   then add   plus
                                     extras?

Recognise if you are an over-researcher (remember the elephant and matchbox, p. 37). This stems from a lack of focus and insecurity about what you are being asked to do. Targeting what you need to research first will massively reduce your workload (see p. 98).

Notice mind wandering 'Mind wandering' can explain why you end up writing an essay that does not answer the question you were asked.

> *Juan, a Fine Art student, wrote Van Gogh's complete life story when he was asked to analyse one of Van Gogh's paintings and say what this told the viewer about Van Gogh's state of mind. Juan realised that his passion about finding out more about Van Gogh took over. As a result he failed.*

Browsing the internet makes mind wandering really easy! So be mindful and notice when this happens – you can waste a lot of time following false lines of enquiry. Keep asking yourself *why* you are doing a task, and *where* what you are doing fits in.

Using the library

Libraries can be quite scary places – but remember they are not like supermarkets, which keep changing where things are on the shelves. Exerting a little effort early on to understand how the library works and where your subject area is will really benefit you.

Your library will do tours. Make sure you take one.

Tips from students include:

Even 2nd or 3rd years can benefit from a tour, as technology changes all the time

Do a repeat tour if needed no-one will notice!

Get to know your subject librarian- they know where the resources for your subject are!

Subject librarians are brilliant because they can:

Do tell them that you are dyslexic and need to target your reading – or they may swamp you with information!

What sort of information should I look for?

This of course depends on your subject, but there are some basic rules:

1 **Use reliable sources** that have been written by established academics in the field. These will have been peer reviewed and checked by other experts to make sure the material included is reliable.

2 **Use journals for up-to-date information**. It is important to know what the current developments in your field are. This is especially important in science and medical subjects where knowledge and practice change fast. *Unless it is an influential text, try to use sources under 10 years old.*

Academic books are peer reviewed so usually reliable, but may not be up to date by the time they are published, **so use journals as well.**

Databases

All universities subscribe to databases, which store thousands of online journals. It is essential you learn how to access and use these to get up-to-date resources. Look at your library information pages and if you get stuck, contact your subject librarian, explain you are dyslexic and ask them to take you through the process.

Keyword searching

Databases are vast, so it can be hard to find what you are looking for. Simple keyword searches will throw up hundreds or thousands of results – or sometimes none!

Write down any words that spring to mind. Use the computer synonyms finder or thesaurus (hover mouse over word and right click) to add to these. Add new keywords you find in abstracts or journal articles (usually near the abstract).

Boolean operators AND, OR and NOT are useful to narrow or widen your search.

This example is from the Boolean Machine: http://kathyschrock.net/rbs3k/boolean/

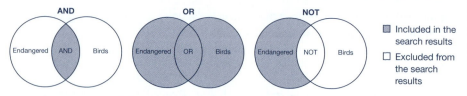

Missing off the end of a word – truncation – widens the search area. For example: using the keyword 'employ' will find 'employee', 'employer' and 'employment'. Some databases use * to indicate this, so enter the keyword employ* to get all the possible endings.

Nobody reads everything!

Reading is acknowledged as an issue for most dyslexics. This section will look at why dyslexics experience difficulty with reading, analyse how *you* tackle reading, and offer a range of strategies for you to try. It starts with a basic reading strategy that fits with your dyslexic learning style, processing LITTLE, but doing this OFTEN. Other ideas will be looked at that suit the different general learning styles (visual, auditory and kinaesthetic – VAK), so bear your individual learning style in mind. You can of course try any of the methods outlined.

No student reads everything on their reading list, however hard they may try. Keeping up with reading is an issue for many students, not just dyslexic ones.

> The trick for all readers is to mimic what effective readers do

Why is reading hard for me? (Or why do I fall asleep!)

Dyslexia is diagnosed when reading, writing and spelling skills are not as good as your ability suggests they should be (assuming there is not another explanation for this, such as missing education as a child). The assessment is likely to have shown that your working memory is weaker and your information processing speed is slower than for non-dyslexics.

As only a few words at a time can be held in your working memory, you may forget the beginning of the sentence by the time you get to the end of it. Academic texts can have long sentences so this leads to lots of re-reading.

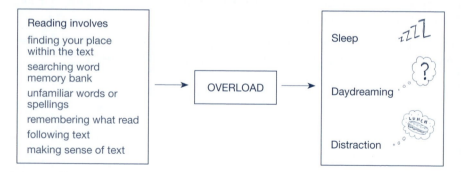

So how do I read?

Reading overloads the dyslexic brain so you end up re-reading, not really understanding what you have read and probably dropping off after 10–20 minutes.

So how do I read? A quick analysis will reveal if you are working with (or against) your dyslexic learning style.

Try this:

▶ Visualise the last text you read. After you selected the book or article, what did you do?
▶ Tick the responses that match best:

What I did	✓ or ✗
Started at the beginning and read to the end	
Started but only got part way through	
Read it all but took ages and kept returning to it	
Read it all in one go	
Left it so late I didn't have time to read any of it	
Got distracted and didn't read it	

Anything else? Did you understand it? Could you explain what the main point was in a couple of sentences without looking back at it? This is not a test, but just to get you thinking about **how you tackle your reading**.

Make any notes here:

What does my reading analysis tell me?

It tells you what you usually do without thinking! It is easy to just start a task without considering why you are doing it, or what you want from it.

If you jump straight in and read everything from start to finish you will soon be over-loaded with information.

This causes:

Now for a bit of honesty. For how long can you *really* read effectively without getting distracted or just reading the words without the information going in? 10 minutes? 15? 20? This will vary with the type of text you are reading, but try to think of this for **your average course reading**.

This is the amount of time it is effective for YOU to read for.

I can read *effectively* for .... minutes.

So what do good readers do?

Don't always read it all

Dip in & out of text

Know which the key bits are before you start reading

Do NOT read every word

If you are dyslexic, reading *every* word in order is like looking at a building by examining every stone – it reveals very little. You need to stand back to get an overview first.

You can mimic what good readers do by looking at the shape of writing and selecting bits of the text to read, using *your* effective reading time.

There are different types of reading – do these help?

Depending on the reading purpose you may choose to:

Scan   Skim   Deep read

Looking for specific words/keywords

Glancing over text for key ideas

Close reading of the text to gain understanding

- *Scanning* requires looking for a particular word in the text.
- *Skimming* involves processing lots of information (fast) and then trying to recall and sift out the important bits.
- *Deep reading* means trying to process information, recall what was written, understand this and link it to previously learnt material in your memory.

If these techniques work for you – use them.

However ... many dyslexics find scanning, skimming and deep reading don't work. This is because they all put extra pressure on your weak processing speed and memory.

This is where metacognition can help. Thinking about the *purpose* of what is being read determinines the strategy used to approach it.

Think before you start reading anything!

Researching for information and then reading it takes a lot of time for dyslexic students at university. Using metacognition and thinking about the purpose of your reading *before* you start will help you reduce the amount you read.

Questions to ask before you start reading

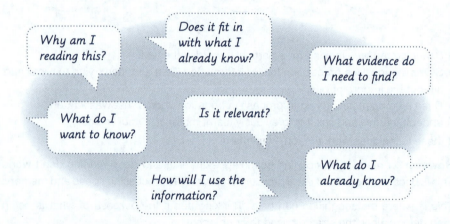

Useful strategies to help stick to the purpose of your reading

1 QUADS

The QUADS grid may be useful to record information from your reading. QUADS stands for *Question, Answer, Detail, Source* (Rose Report, 2009).

QUestion	**A**nswer	**D**etail	**S**ource

2 SQ3R

Survey, Question, Read, Recall and then *Review* later.

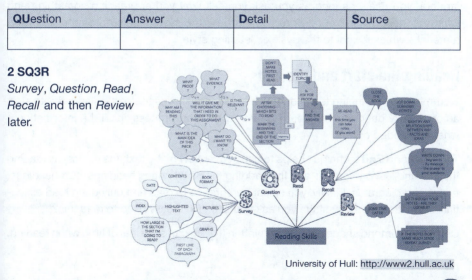

University of Hull: http://www2.hull.ac.uk

3 The Cornell note-taking system

Record, *Question* (then later on *Recite*, *Reflect* and *Review*). See pp. 34–6 for details.

Notice that all these techniques encourage thinking about what you want to find out before you waste valuable time just reading anything you find. It does not matter which strategy you use – as long as you ask yourself *why* you are reading something and *what* you need to find out before you start. All the systems also promote *reviewing* material – which is vital to the dyslexic learning style.

Reading the start and the end

Skimming and scanning techniques are hard for dyslexics to do. It is very easy to start automatically deep reading (reading every word and processing all the information – whether needed or not).

The **Start and End** technique helps to get an overview of the text (the basics) by reading the first and last paragraphs and then adding to this by noting headings, sub-headings, tables and diagrams. Finally, you select paragraphs to read and only deep read essential information. At every stage you ask yourself: 'Do I really *need* to read this?'

Using the diamond shape of anything written (p. 72) can save lots of time when reading.

Stage 1   *Read the start and end only*

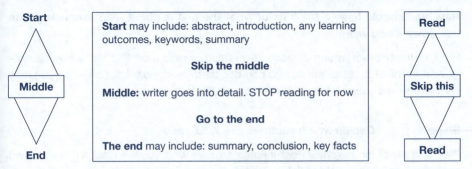

Start may include: abstract, introduction, any learning outcomes, keywords, summary

Skip the middle

Middle: writer goes into detail. STOP reading for now

Go to the end

The end may include: summary, conclusion, key facts

Stage 2   *Flick through the middle*

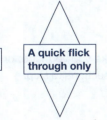

Notice

- ▶ Headings and sub-headings
- ▶ Graphics – diagrams, tables, charts, graphs, figures
- ▶ Other types of info – case history, examples
- ▶ Any key points highlighted or mini summaries; look in margins or for boxes

Stage 3   *STOP – Consider if you need to read any more*

Now, you should have a fair idea of what the text is about – an overview. Write this down if you wish.

Get into the habit of asking yourself: *'Do I need to read more?'* If the answer is no – leave it for now! It still exists so you can decide to read more later on – but you may just have saved yourself time and effort by asking this question.

Stage 4   *Decide which sections you WILL read*

Pick up a pencil (or use small Post-it notes) to mark what you will read. If it is your own copy of a book it may help to lightly mark in the margin by the text:

✓   must read

✗   don't think needed

?   not sure

If you are using a library book rub out any pencil marks you've made; or you could scan and print, photocopy or just mentally note which sections to skip.

This is what Catherine's article looked like after she did this (note: you only have to mark the text in the margins!):

You can see now that Catherine has to read much less than she originally thought.

This simple technique can reduce your reading load at a pencil stroke!

Stage 5   Ask yourself again, 'Do I need to read more?'

Being selective will conserve your energy and work better with your dyslexic learning style.

Stage 6   Read the start of selected paragraphs

By selectively reading the beginning of paragraphs you will get the main idea. It will depend on your purpose whether you need to read the detail. Bear in mind you may not need the precise detail anyway.

| **Stage 7** | **Ask yourself again, 'Do I need to read more?'** |
| **Stage 8** | **Only now consider reading the text in detail. This is DEEP READING** (see p. 55). |

Every paragraph should contain one idea which is developed. The first sentences usually indicate the main idea. Following sentences provide evidence, examples or arguments to support or dismiss the main idea.

Only deep read when you need detailed information. It takes time and effort and you may have to re-read it several times before you understand it. Learn to be mindful about *when* you deep read and don't just automatically fall into deep reading.

When you decide to deep read, read the text in short chunks, stopping as soon as you get sleepy or distracted as this indicates you are working beyond your memory and processing capacity. Take a break and come back to it later.

Why the Start and End method is good for dyslexic readers

This is because you use your maximum concentration time to learn a bit more depth each time you revisit the article. Doing this in short bursts means you start the process of over-learning, but do not overload your memory or processing capacity.

Other reading strategies

Reading journals or chapters using the Start and End method fits in with the LITTLE and OFTEN dyslexia learning style, but you also have a personal learning style (VAK). There are other reading strategies that can capitalise on your individual learning style.

Learning style	Reading strategy
Visual	Use software that highlights text as it is read out (text-to-speech software can do this). Also try textmapping (p. 64).
Auditory	Convert text to a sound file using assistive technology (text-to-speech software). Listen to recordings, read aloud or listen to someone else reading aloud.
Kinaesthetic	Read aloud, listen to recording whilst doing something else (driving, walking).

Using assistive technology to help with reading

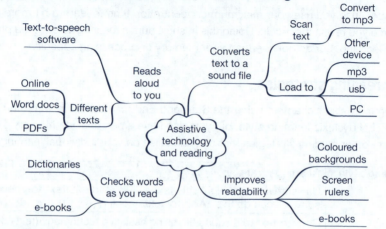

Text-to-speech software

Reads aloud to you

Different texts
- Online
- Word docs
- PDFs

Converts text to a sound file
- Scan text
- Load to

Convert to mp3

Other device
- mp3
- usb
- PC

Assistive technology and reading

Checks words as you read
- Dictionaries
- e-books

Improves readability
- Coloured backgrounds
- Screen rulers
- e-books

Textmapping

Textmapping helps visual and/or kinaesthetic learners to engage with the text in an interactive way (developed by R. David Middlebrook, 1990):

Photocopy or print off the text onto single-sided paper

Join it all together in one whole piece

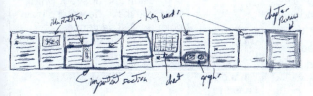

Map the text using your own system of colours and notes. This encourages you to 'see' the text as a whole and not get stuck in the detail you will not remember in the middle.

Roll it up and store as a scroll

Concentrate on beginnings and endings (introduction and conclusion); then starts and ends of sections to focus on the main ideas.

For more information on textmapping see www.textmapping.org/

Taking notes from reading

When making notes from reading it is easy to start writing (or highlighting) too much. This is a sign you have fallen into deep reading.

Try not to make notes until after you have read the introduction and any conclusion (and abstract if there is one) using any of the reading strategies outlined (Start and End, textmapping, text to speech).

Then try to write:

▶ What you think the main idea is
▶ Why you think this is important
▶ How you can use it.

You may find it useful to do this at the top of any notes you make:

Date	Notes
Full ref	
Find out	1. 2. 3.
What about	After you have read introduction, conclusion and abstract write what you think the writer's main point is. 2–3 sentences
Why important	
What do I need to know?	
	Now you can start to take brief notes
Summary	Leave space to do this later ...

Consider if you need to know anything else – go back to any questions you wrote down.

Find the answer to any new questions you think of. Write this down.

Any other questions???

Visual stress: using coloured backgrounds can help

Some dyslexics also suffer from visual stress when reading. Lines of text may be blurred or appear to move and the white spaces on a page may glare.

Visual stress is called Mearles–Irlen syndrome, scotopic sensitivity syndrome or visual dyslexia. Up to 20% of people may benefit from using coloured backgrounds when reading. This can reduce glare and increase concentration.

For books: use coloured filters, overlays or tinted glasses

For printed copies: try coloured paper

For computer screens: change the display background or the colour of the font

These simple measures can have a dramatic effect on your reading speed and comprehension. They are well worth trying, but may not work for all dyslexics.

Why is writing hard for me?
(Or, I know it but can't get it down on paper)

Every dyslexic student experiences this. However well you know your material it seems impossible to get it down on paper.

If you are dyslexic:

Ideas flash in and out of your mind.
You put off the dreaded moment of actually starting to write by reading a lot.
You have lots of ideas all competing for your attention.
Ideas will just come tumbling out randomly.
No time to re-order your ideas, or you are unsure which ideas to develop.

... which results in these sort of comments:

Interesting points but lacks analysis.

Lots of good ideas, but lacks structure.

Unfortunately, a confused writer leads to a confused reader, and lower marks.

> Planning is essential to avoid confusing both yourself and your reader!

Planning is positive! (and reduces your workload)

Planning …

Gives you an overview

Sorts out your thoughts

Makes you look at different views

Eliminates unnecessary material

Shows up where you have lack of evidence

Identifies areas where you need to research and fill in gaps

Allows you to break the task down into manageable chunks

Fits into the dyslexic learning style

Keeps you on track …

Some very simple planning will save a lot of time and trouble.

Ideally, your essay will go straight from the introduction, through a series of logical steps, to the conclusion:

Introduction

Logical steps

A clear conclusion

Unfortunately, many students' assignments end up looking like this:

Introduction

Muddled middle

No clear conclusion

Planning helps avoid this result by breaking the task down into manageable chunks.

First plan (pre-planning)

Collect: Blank computer page or paper (A3 if possible) and pencil, coloured pens or highlighters.

OK, go! Write, anything ... Spend a few minutes just getting down *any* ideas that occur to you. Bullet point ideas, mind map or just randomly write.

Don't worry about sorting ideas out for the moment, just get them down.

Next:

1 Mark your work with a ✓ (or Y for Yes if typing), X or ?

✓ or Y if typing   anything that you *must* include

✗   anything that does not seem to fit in, or you can't find information (evidence) about

?   anything you are not sure about or would like to include but may not have room for

2 Colour code anything you think goes together: just circle or strike through the word or highlight or change the font colour if typing.

You now have a basic plan of ideas you may develop. Each colour should represent one idea.

This can be turned into your assignment! Later ideas can be added in a different colour.

This is your first plan – see p. 76 for developing your plan.

The shape of anything written!

Any well-written text has a diamond shape!

Introduction

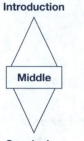

Middle

Conclusion

> **Introduction** Tells the reader why the subject is important and how the author will deal with it.
>
> **Middle** Consists of a series of steps examining the subject
>
> *leading to*
>
> **Conclusion** Discusses where it went and any implication of this

This applies to all kinds of writing: essays, reports, chapters in books and dissertations. Remembering this will improve the structure of whatever you are writing.

Shape your assignment

Before doing any planning, 'shape' your assignment. First, make your work fit within any word count or page count. It is *much* easier to do this at the start than have to rewrite at the end to make it fit.

A bit of basic maths is all you need. For a 2000-word assignment:

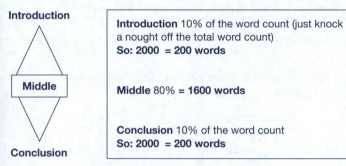

Introduction

Middle

Conclusion

Introduction 10% of the word count (just knock a nought off the total word count)
So: 2000 = 200 words

Middle 80% = 1600 words

Conclusion 10% of the word count
So: 2000 = 200 words

Dividing up the middle – 1600 words

Look at your colour-coded pre-planning; each colour should be one theme to develop.

If you have 4 themes, divide the middle word count by 4.

1600/4 = 400 words for each section

You do not have to use exactly 400 words for each section; this is a just a guide to start off with.

Word counts are useful: they tell you how much (or, even better, how little) research you need to do.

> The word count is your budget. Stick to it! (it takes a lot of time to adjust this at the end if you have written too much)

Planning tools

With your word count in mind you can develop your plan. The planning tool you use to do this is your choice. Here are some suggestions:

Boxes   Mindmapping

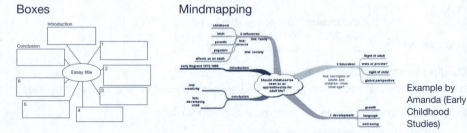

Example by Amanda (Early Childhood Studies)

PowerPoint slides

Table or matrix

Point	Evidence	Example	So...

Post-it notes (the computer version is Stickies)

... or anything else you think will work for you. Think back: is there something you did in the past that worked well for you? Don't think that now you are a university student this may not work for you any more. You may have to adapt it, of course.

Lucy's friend helped her out when he made her a Word document with text boxes in it and told her she could only write about one thing in each box. Brilliantly simple – but this enabled Lucy to write perfect paragraphs.

Developing your plan

It is best to first FRAME and then FILL in your plan. Don't worry about having all the information needed to write the assignment. The gaps can be filled in later.

Frame and Fill is when you have your first plan (see pp. 70–1) and use this as an outline (or frame) for your assignment. This means you just start with a series of headings to which you add later.

Arrabella's mind map can be turned into a framework for her essay:

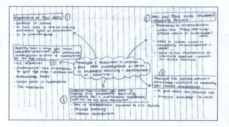

converted to a

1 Importance of fair tests
- sciences is...
- A Challenging
2 How fair tests take children's ...
- Ref to construc ...
- etc.
3 Analyse the process....
- Good lesson LO
- Subject knowledge
- etc

Mind map

framework for her essay

Most mind-mapping software can also do this for you. You make a mind map and the software programme can convert this to a linear outline (your frame!).

Carol (Foundation Ministry) used Inspiration software to produce her mind map and a linear framework for her to 'fill in'.

Each idea (represented on your plan by a mind map branch, Post-it note, PowerPoint slide, or box) now needs to be turned into a paragraph.

What is where in the assignment?

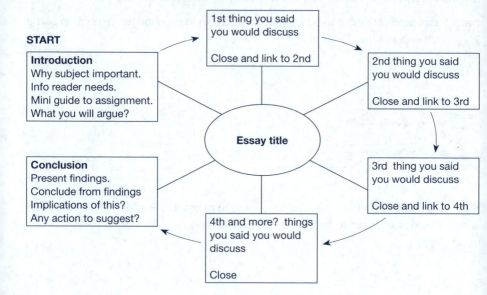

START

Introduction
Why subject important.
Info reader needs.
Mini guide to assignment.
What you will argue?

Conclusion
Present findings.
Conclude from findings
Implications of this?
Any action to suggest?

Essay title

1st thing you said
you would discuss

Close and link to 2nd

2nd thing you said
you would discuss

Close and link to 3rd

3rd thing you said
you would discuss

Close and link to 4th

4th and more? things
you said you would
discuss

Close

Notice that the introduction and conclusion are side by side. These should 'mirror' each other. Put these side by side when you write the conclusion so you can clearly see where everything you said you would do in the introduction went.

What should be in a paragraph?

Every paragraph should develop ONE point only. Each paragraph also follows the diamond structure.

Open Clearly indicate the idea to be discussed (what paragraph is about, the point you will develop)

Middle Provide supporting evidence for (and maybe against) your point

Close and link Where are you now? Can you show how this links to the question? Are there any implications? (This is where you show *your* voice in the paragraph.)

Paragraph checker

Use WEED to check that the paragraph is complete.

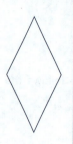

What: Is it clear what point you will develop?

Evidence: The main point must be supported (or questioned) using evidence from your reading and research. (So every paragraph should contain at least one reference and usually more.)

Example: Is an example needed? (Not always.)

Do: So what? What will you do with this now? Can you show how this links to the question?

Paragraph showing WEED

W = What

E = Evidence

E = Example (not always needed)

D = Do

Transition is the inner movement or journey we make in reaction to a change. Lewin's (1951) model of change management describes the need to unfreeze, change and refreeze the organisation in order to continue with the change and prevent regression to the former systems. In order to help the junior members of the team, leaders were attempting to provide education and staff support; this has been difficult at times due to lack of staff and time. The team may have not become so disheartened and split if the Trust had acknowledged the need for financial investment to support the change. Hayes (2008 p179) states, "the key to modernisation is the need to change attitudes and culture within the health care service". Therefore leadership using the best strategies for the type of change may help influence staff to work towards the change.

(Julie, Healthcare)

How long should a paragraph be?

Your poor reader cannot concentrate for a whole page of dense text (and neither can you!). Do the 'upside down test' to see if your paragraphs are too long:

Print your work out (single-sided is best). Lay it out *upside down*.

You should see clear blocks (one block = one paragraph which develops one point).

If it looks like this, the paragraphs need sorting out:

STUDYING WITH DYSLEXIA

Do the paragraph hand test: hold your hand up and spread your thumb and first finger out. Keep your paragraphs no longer than that!

So, about two paragraphs per page ...

(With thanks to Kate Williams 2011)

Using assistive technology to help writing

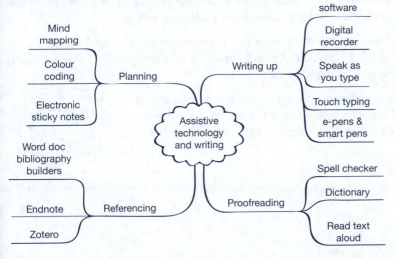

Assistive technology and writing

- Planning
  - Mind mapping
  - Colour coding
  - Electronic sticky notes
- Writing up
  - software
  - Digital recorder
  - Speak as you type
  - Touch typing
  - e-pens & smart pens
- Referencing
  - Word doc bibliography builders
  - Endnote
  - Zotero
- Proofreading
  - Spell checker
  - Dictionary
  - Read text aloud

Touch typing – why it is a good idea

When you are writing there is a lot going on. You are having to:

Recall   Reword   Rework information   AND   Remember it while you write it down

Being dyslexic makes remembering and processing information much harder than for non-dyslexics, and the act of writing adds in another process. This simply overloads everything so that you lose track of what you were trying to say.

Touch typing means that one of these processes becomes automatic so you do not have to think about it consciously. This lightens the load, and students who can touch type report that it helps significantly.

It is well worth the effort of learning to touch type. You can find 'typing tutor' software online (but do check if your university has one available first): www.dyslexic.com/index.asp?url=IND

touch typing

Referencing is harder if you are dyslexic

You find …

Referencing needs extra care and generally takes longer than you expect it to.

Referencing – using your computer

Try these ...

Use Word to build your bibliography. For Harvard use APA.

Use referencing software such as Endnote to build your references. Good for dissertations. **Zotero** is a free online alternative.

Colour code sections of your work for different sources. *All information from book by Smith in red. Article by Jones in blue.* Make sure you note colour used for different sources!

Create your own mini referencing guide. Copy and paste from uni online guides. Copy examples into your work so you can follow the correct style. Remember to delete the example!

Start your mini guide with:
- Book
- Journal
- Journal accessed from a database
- Web articles

Add other examples as you use them.

TOP TIP Add in your references as you go. Save yourself from a horrible job at the end!

Colour coding references

You could colour code your reference guide if you think it would help sequence the information.

Author (date) title edition? Place: Publisher

Godwin J (2009). Planning your essay (2nd edn). Basingstoke: Palgrave Macmillan.

The book pages below show where the reference information was found on the book title pages.

Use your mobile to photograph the book cover and title pages so you have all the information needed for the reference.

Plagiarism

Plagiarism is when you use someone else's work (or idea) in your assignment and don't make it clear where you got it from. This means you are presenting it as your idea, even if you didn't mean to.

Avoiding plagiarism is easy once you understand when you have to reference.

How do I know what should be referenced and what shouldn't?

Ask yourself:

Question	Comment	Do I have to reference it?
Did you have to read it to know it?	Where did you find it? If you read it somewhere you should reference it.	Yes
Is it your own idea?	If your idea has developed from the evidence you have already referenced you don't need to reference it again. This is your idea.	No. Your reader can see that you have progressed from the (referenced) research. Worth extra marks as this puts 'your voice' into your work.

How do I know what should be referenced and what shouldn't? (cont.)

Question	Comment	Do I have to reference it?
Is it your own idea?	Are you sure you didn't find it out somewhere?	Probably. Unless you are asked to present your original ideas it is best to avoid this.
Does everybody know it?	No need to reference it then.	No
Is it common knowledge in your subject area?	No need to reference it; it may be hard to find out whose idea it originally was.	No, but if in doubt reference it.
How do I know this?	You didn't just wake up knowing this!	Probably
Did you put someone's idea into your own words?	It is still their idea.	Yes
Did you quote directly?	You must also include the page number.	Yes (include page number).

The golden rule is: If in doubt, reference it.

Avoiding plagiarism

Follow this good practice and you will avoid plagiarism:

▸ Allow plenty of time to do your work – it is tempting to copy if you are rushing.
▸ Make a note of where you find information.
▸ When taking notes record the full reference at the top of the page.
▸ When paraphrasing try not to look back at the original until you have written it down; then check it is correct.

Paraphrasing – putting it in YOUR own words

You can use exactly the same words as the author if you reference it as a direct quote: **'if you do this you must reference it correctly AND add the page number' (Godwin 2012 pxx).**

Quoting, however, only shows your reader you found it, not that you understood it. So you always need to explain a quote. When you put it into your own words you demonstrate you truly 'got it'.

Or you can put it into your own words by paraphrasing. This of course is not always easy – you may like the way the writer put it and feel they said it perfectly.

Paraphrasing should **summarise** information and **show you understood it**.

Try this technique:

- Read the passage – try to work out the main idea.
- Write down 4 or 5 main words from it on a separate piece of paper. Can you change any of them? If so, cross out the original one and use the new one.
- Leave it for a few minutes.
- Try to write it in your own words.
- Check the main idea is the same – if not, repeat the process.
- Check you have not used exactly the same words.

Summarising by paraphrasing is hard, but the benefit is that you really learn your stuff; this will show in your work and grades.

8   Checking everything

Proofreading tips

Let's be honest, this is never going to be a strong point of yours. But there are times you cannot avoid this. These tips will help with the main issues.

- **Write short sentences** – this helps you keep track of what you are saying.
- **Read it out loud** – or get a friend to read it to you. You will often be able to hear mistakes you cannot see. Or use assistive technology text-to-speech software to do this for you.
- **Spelling** – try to pick the right one, of course, but then be consistent. Your reader will forgive an error, but swapping between versions will just get on their nerves.

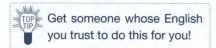
Get someone whose English you trust to do this for you!

Spelling – why it is an issue and how you can cope with this

Spelling will usually be a problem if you are dyslexic. This is because your memory and processing difficulties interfered with your ability to process phonological information when you where learning to read, and may still do so. It means your spelling can be erratic and vary from day to day. When you are stressed or working to a deadline your spelling may be much worse than usual.

Some students find these helpful …

Computer spell checker If you get a red wiggly line under a word, then check it. Right clicking should come up with suggestions to start with. A green wiggly line is a grammatical error. Unless it changes your meaning, go with it; it is usually correct.

Keep a spelling book Circle spellings in your work you suspect are wrong. When you have found the correct spellings enter them in your spelling book. (An address book is good for this.) Add a brief explanation or you will be looking it up again. Beware of false friends, though – when a word has different meanings and may have a different spelling too. Example: to, too and two.

Keeping a spelling book does not suit everyone, so only do this if it helps.

Assistive technology Spell checkers and dictionaries in assistive technology programs are much better than ordinary spell checkers for Word documents. So run your work through these before handing it in. They also build up knowledge of the correct spellings for the words you use most often and will autocorrect words.

Online dictionaries You can try online dictionaries such as dictionary.com. Beware using the thesaurus, though, if you are at all unsure of the meaning. You may be saying something very different to what you meant! Specialist online dictionaries can be very useful, so try to locate one for your subject.

e-books – These may have a facility to check the meaning of words.

Use MUSP to learn your spellings

Everyone has spellings they find difficult. At university you are coming across new words every day. You cannot learn all the new spellings at once, but if you tackle 4–6 a week using Jenny Lee's MUSP system http://cw.routledge.com/textbooks/9780415597562/spelling5.asp you will soon build up a bank of words you commonly use that you can spell.

MUSP stands for **M**ulti **S**ensory **S**pelling **P**rogramme. MUSP uses over-learning and a range of techniques – visual, auditory and kinaesthetic – which fit in with your dyslexic and individual learning style.

Try to review and practise 4–6 spellings a week. Continue reviewing spellings for about a month, then review at intervals just to make sure you can still recall the spelling. If you start to misspell the word again just add it to the weekly list.

Pick a word you misspell and try the MUSP method.

The MUSP method explained

What to do ...	An example ...
Pick a word you know you misspell Write it out a few times. It doesn't matter if you misspell it several ways.	elephent elephaint elephant elefant
Find the correct spelling – use a dictionary, textbook or spell checker	elephant
Identify where the error occurs – underline this, notice the correct way.	eleph<u>ent</u>
Choose a strategy – to help you remember the correct way to spell the word. You can be creative here.	an eleph<u>ant</u> stepping on an ant
LOOK at the word and strategy	

SAY the word and strategy	
COVER the word and strategy	
SAY the word and strategy, **PICTURE** each part in your mind	
SAY the strategy as you **WRITE** the word	*"The elephant steps on the ant"*
CHECK	
Adapted from Jenny Lee's (2000) MUSP spelling programme for priority words.	

Repeat this process with different words until you have a short list (no more than 10 new words a week). Practise your list daily using the MUSP technique. Drop words from the list once you are confident you can spell them correctly.

Memory (and forgetting)

Everyone forgets what they have learnt if they don't review it later on.

The good news is that once you have learnt it thoroughly it stays with you in your long-term memory. The trick is learning it well enough for this to happen.

This graph represents how much is forgotten without reviewing (80%) and how much remembered when reviewed (100%). This is why the Cornell note-taking system works – it builds in regular reviewing (see pp. 34–6).

The forgetting (and remembering) curve

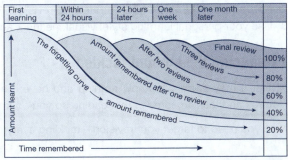

Westminster School (no date)

In dyslexia this process is slower and not as sure because your short-term memory and slower speed of processing mean everything takes much longer.

So you need to start earlier – and be clever about how you tackle your revision to suit your dyslexic learning style. Review the pages on short-term memory and dyslexia learning style so you 'review' why doing LITTLE and OFTEN helps (see pp. 5–6).

Tackling revision in a dyslexia-friendly way

There are 3 things to consider here:
1 Reduce the amount tackled.
2 Apply the LITTLE and OFTEN strategy to revision.
3 Use your personal learning style: visual, hearing, active (or a bit of each!)

1 Reducing the amount tackled

At first it may seem you know nothing and have it all to do. But you have been to lectures and tackled some of the reading so you *do* know something already.

Now you need to target your revision – tackling everything is impossible.

Firstly, only learn off by heart essential information such as names, dates and formulas. Then concentrate on understanding the main concepts or ideas so you can demonstrate your understanding.

Secondly, look through your course information – it may help to do a mind map of what was covered each week. Have a look at past papers quickly if you have them. Which topics are more likely to come up? Did you have any clues from tutors? Target these first.

Thirdly, make a note any of gaps in your notes you need to fill. Do these as soon as you can. Then have a go at planning answers to any questions you have (past papers or mock exams) or make up your own questions.

Set yourself clear targets – a 'to do' list is useful for this and will help you monitor your progress. Sometimes you have to make a 'strategic decision' to miss a topic out due to lack of time.

Amber (a foundation Science student) knew there was no way she could get her head round the genetics topic in time for the exam, so she abandoned it and revised her 3 other topics better – a calculated risk that paid off.

2 Applying LITTLE and OFTEN

In the panic of revision it is easy to forget to use the LITTLE and OFTEN learning style which helps deal with the dyslexic issues of memory and over-learning. Try to work out how long you can work efficiently for different activities and stick to this.

- Most importantly, STOP or switch activity when you notice your attention is drifting.
- Work out when you work best – and save tough topics for then (see p. 16) .

Taking mini breaks is *vital*

If you are dyslexic you need to take lots of breaks so you don't overload too much. Even when you are not working your brain is still trying to make sense of things. Do you sometimes wake up with a solution to a problem? Your hardworking brain was hard at it while you slept! Be confident: mini breaks mean more is learnt in the end …

Keeping going ...

Have lots of mini treats lined up (and some bigger ones for time off).

Mini treat	Chocolate bar or luxury coffee, a 10-minute walk, the gym, a phone call, cook a favourite meal … Your suggestions?
Bigger treat	The cinema, a long walk, a meal out … Your suggestions?

Try not to revise up to the last minute.

Joe, doing Law, always took the night off before an exam. He went to a concert, play or film and was still fresh for the exam. Joe said working till the last minute didn't give enough time 'for it to sink in'.

When should I start?

As soon as you can! If you get into the habit of constantly reviewing work then revision will be much easier to deal with. So if you know you have an exam, try to:

Same day as lectures	Review notes later the same day or ASAP. Use Cornell (pp. 34–6) or summarise on a sticky note or Post-it note.
Within a week	Review summary, note in review column/margin any missing info or questions you have – use a different colour so you can spot additions easily.

Within 3 weeks	If it is a likely exam topic: follow up any missing notes and find past papers – are there any questions on this topic? If so, start some active revision – whatever you like: cards, mind map, recording or talking aloud.
Until you start seriously revising	Continue reviewing everything – at least glance through it weekly and more often if possible. Even brief reviewing will help.

Revision timetables – to do or not to do?

A too strict revision timetable can be unhelpful. It is a bit like following a diet: if you slip up and fail to hit your target you get fed up with yourself and may give up.

Try to make any timetable realistic. A mini slip-up is OK, it is human! Just keep going. Dyslexia means it takes longer to do things, *not* that you can't do it.

If a revision timetable has helped before, do this, but include lots of mini breaks.

Time	Mon	Tue	Wed	Thurs	Fri	Sat	Sun
9		Make list Soc topics	Psychol wk 7-9			Practice paper	
10	Gym	Select topics, find notes		Library - get past papers	Gym		
11		Look up SD	Meet group				
12	Stats, find notes	Lunch	Plan essay	Stats 2 topics review	Review notes		
1	Walk	Mock	Lunch Emma				
2	Psychol Wk 1-3 notes review	Mock	Mind map Soc module	Café - Joe		Travel	
3		Mock	Find Soc books	Practise Paper 2 notes		Football	
4	Call home	Coffee	Walk			Football	
5	Cook	Psychol Wk 4-6	Notes for Q3	Swim		Football	
6	'To do' list for week	Write Q	Cook	Stat Chap 2		Travel	
7	Stats notes Find gaps	Shop	Select 3 topics, find exam Q	Film night		Review past paper	
8		Cook	Plan 1 Q				
9		Topics for 2mw	Drink with Dan				

But if this seems too regimented, a simple list may work just as well.

Example:

Time	Activity
20 mins	Collect notes on ....
20 mins	Write out possible questions for ....
10 mins	Tidy up room
20 mins	Plan brief answer for 1 question
20 mins	Check against notes/textbook, highlight problem bits
20 mins	Break

Don't spend hours on this – it is a tool and does not have to look pretty!

3 Using what works best for your learning style

You can use any of these:

- ▶ visual – by seeing
- ▶ auditory – by hearing/listening
- ▶ kinaesthetic – by doing (action or movement)

… or a mixture of all of them – try whatever works for you.

Amount recalled when reading, listening, seeing, speaking and doing

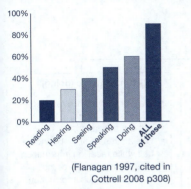

(Flanagan 1997, cited in Cottrell 2008 p308)

… so mixing and matching these activities is a good idea!

Don't dismiss what has worked for you in the past – just adapt it …

> *Joe, a Law student, used different coloured cards (and shapes) to distinguish between criminal law and tort in order to learn 200+ cases. Despite his very slow processing Joe was the only student on the course to do this … and he got a First.*

The message here is be inventive about revision: ***don't just read.*** Be ACTIVE in your revision!

Revising actively – what could you use?

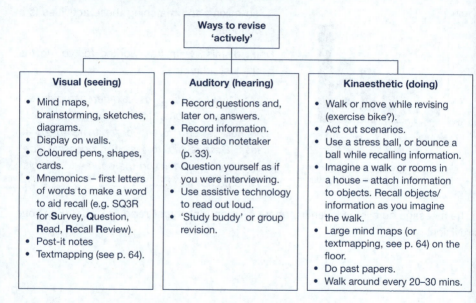

Ways to revise 'actively'

Visual (seeing)

- Mind maps, brainstorming, sketches, diagrams.
- Display on walls.
- Coloured pens, shapes, cards.
- Mnemonics – first letters of words to make a word to aid recall (e.g. SQ3R for **S**urvey, **Q**uestion, **R**ead, **R**ecall **R**eview).
- Post-it notes
- Textmapping (see p. 64).

Auditory (hearing)

- Record questions and, later on, answers.
- Record information.
- Use audio notetaker (p. 33).
- Question yourself as if you were interviewing.
- Use assistive technology to read out loud.
- 'Study buddy' or group revision.

Kinaesthetic (doing)

- Walk or move while revising (exercise bike?).
- Act out scenarios.
- Use a stress ball, or bounce a ball while recalling information.
- Imagine a walk or rooms in a house – attach information to objects. Recall objects/information as you imagine the walk.
- Large mind maps (or textmapping, see p. 64) on the floor.
- Do past papers.
- Walk around every 20–30 mins.

You can of course use a mixture of these – but do use some of them.

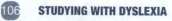

Dealing with distractions – what will be your strategy?

Don't worry about short distractions – 10 minutes or so – these are helpful for your dyslexic learning style. But if you are taking more breaks than working then consider how to change this.

Distractions will happen sometimes! What are your most common distractions?

- Social media
- ?
- ?

If you are constantly on the internet and social media, use this as a reward after a period of study:

> 1 hour study time = 10 mins online.

Some sites can monitor how you spend your time – this may be a revelation!

Think ahead how to deal with distractions: *"I can meet for coffee, but not a night out this week."*

Or make it work for YOU!

> *Abdullah realised he was doing a lot of his friend's revision for him by chatting on social media. He made this work for him by only discussing areas he needed to cover, so getting his own work done at the same time.*

Be kind to yourself

Exams are stressful, so make sure you eat and sleep as well as you can. Being tired or feeling sluggish because of a bad diet won't help.

Stress is normal and, under control, even helpful. Keeping as stress-free as possible will reduce the impact of dyslexia.

If it is all getting out of hand …

Do contact your university support service if you are over-stressed or dealing with your stress in an unhelpful way, such as avoiding work or using alcohol or drugs.

Your mental and physical health comes first. Don't be scared to seek help if you need to. Check online to see what help is available at your university or college.

> Exams are important – but it is not the end of the world if you fail one.

The night before an exam

What to do	Check you have:
Set your alarm	At least one, and the sound is on!
Pack	What you need (pen, ruler, calculator etc.)
Check	Time. Place. How long for?
Check exam format if you can	Worked out possible times per question.
Eat	Eaten properly! Something to eat for breakfast?
Know what time to leave home	Added enough time for it to go wrong!
Know how to travel there	Checked any timetables and have enough money for fares.
Sleep	Set the alarm …

Try to relax, get as much sleep as possible. Avoid last-minute revision.

Why do I find exams so difficult?

The combination of these 'ingredients' in the exam makes it hard for you to produce accurate, clearly structured answers within the time allowed.

Many dyslexic students try to choose units of study that are *not* assessed by exam, or where the exam is only part of the assessment. Avoiding exams is not always possible, though, as many courses have in-class tests or practical-based assessments.

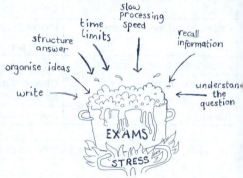

You should be entitled to 25% extra time if you have had a full dyslexia assessment and a Special Needs assessment (see p. 130) which details any extra support provisions available to you.

Extra time and other exam provisions

Most dyslexic students get 25% extra time allowed for exams.

25% = 15 minutes extra time for each hour of the exam.

This to compensate for the longer time it takes you to process the written information on the exam paper and recall, sequence and write down your answer.

You may also be allocated an exam room with other SpLD students. This may be a smaller room with less noise and distractions than large exam halls.

Depending on what is recommended in your Special Needs assessment (see p. 130), you may also be allowed to use a computer or even a scribe in the exam.

Research shows stress increases the effect of dyslexia. This includes crunch times such as coursework deadlines or exams.

Learn to use your extra time constructively, gain marks and be less stressed in the exam.

Thinking back over past exam performance

This will be helpful to improve your future exam performance. So be honest!

Tick any of these you know have happened to you:

What happened?	✓ or X	See page
Ran out of time		p. 116
Wrote down everything I could think of		p. 118
Gave short answer then got stuck		pp. 117, 118, 119
Missed out part of the question		pp. 117, 118, 119

These are costing you marks … so read on.

Other problems are:

▸ answering the wrong number of questions
▸ wrongly numbering questions on the answer paper.

These are typical dyslexic errors so double- and triple-check for these.

Running out of time

Time management in the exam is vital – usually it takes longer than you thought to answer questions.

Strictly work out how much time you have for each question and stick to this.

You always pick up more marks if you attempt ALL the required questions. Most marks are gained at the start of your answer and tail off as you start to repeat or include irrelevant information.

Writing down everything you know about a subject

You just start to write down everything you can recall about that subject.

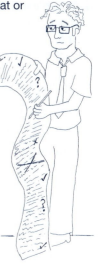

This is caused by a lack of confidence in what the question actually means. Time spent analysing the question will be well spent (p. 117)

Giving too short answers – your answers are not detailed enough

The problem here is not developing an answer – answering the question but not providing supporting evidence. The examiner wants you to show the thinking behind your answer.

Try these ways to develop your answer:

▶ Useful questions such as the 5 W's: **W**hat, **W**hy, **W**hen, **W**here and **W**ho (and **H**ow!) can help.

▶ Ask yourself why the examiner asked the question. Usually it is so you can:
show your knowledge and understanding
and
apply this to an imaginary scenario

Missing out part of the question

Two-part (or more) questions are tricky. It is easy to start answering the first part of the question, which may seem quite simple, then forget to do the other parts …

Example:

Outline the key issues … . Select one key issue you have discussed and … .

1st part: Outline … show you know the main ideas

2nd part: analytical, focuses on 1 or 2 issues in depth

So:

1st part of question

2nd part of question

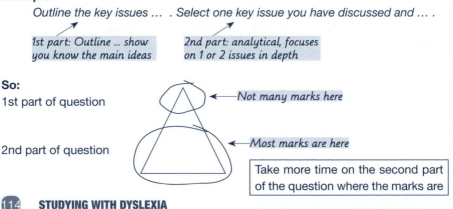

Not many marks here

Most marks are here

Take more time on the second part of the question where the marks are

Answering the wrong number of questions

It happens! Check and double-check.

In her law exam Fatima answered all 8 questions, when she was asked to only do 3. It was a 2-hour exam (so she had 2 ½ hours with her extra time). Despite all her efforts she failed. Obviously she could not give enough detail in 15–20 minutes per question when she should really have allowed herself 40–50 minutes for each one.

A note about proofreading

If you really think proofreading will get you extra marks, leave 10 minutes at the end for this.

BUT – for most dyslexics proofreading does not work, so in an exam don't bother.

Reasons proofreading may not work for you:
▶ Spelling errors are hard to spot.
▶ You may change something you were sure of when you wrote it and thus alter the meaning.
Have the confidence to leave it alone!

Still, **always check your work** for errors, particularly in science, maths and multiple choice questions.

Using your extra time constructively

The extra time is useful because it:

▶ reduces stress
▶ allows time to plan or structure your answer.

Avoid making the same old errors by first checking you know how to tackle any problem areas you have (see p. 112). Next, consider how to use your extra time more constructively in future.

Give yourself permission to use the extra time to:

▶ work out your timings in the exam
▶ analyse the question
▶ plan your answer.

These are real time savers, so don't be tempted just to start writing. It will cost you more time in the end.

Work out your timings in the exam

Carefully check you have selected the right number of questions, and decide which order to do them in.

Analysing the question

Helpful types of words in the question:

Word type	Example	Function
Process (sometimes called the instruction, direction or keyword)	Discuss, evaluate, critically analyse, briefly outline	Tells you the process you have to do; also indicates depth of research required
Subject or content	The main area under discussion	Broad focus of answer (try to stick to this only)
Limit or scope	Dates, geographical area, number of examples	Focuses the area to be examined; note this carefully
Other **significant** words – key aspects	Any other aspects not covered above	Pinpointing limit or scope of answer

Adapted from Williams (1995).

Use highlighters to identify the different types of words in the question:

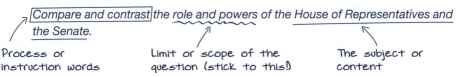

Compare and contrast the role and powers of the House of Representatives and the Senate.

Process or instruction words

Limit or scope of the question (stick to this!)

The subject or content

Planning your answer in the exam

You can use any methods you feel happy with: mind map, bullet points, table/matrix (see pp. 74–5) for more). Decide if you want to plan all the answers first or one by one as you tackle them.

For each question:

1 Take a few minutes to write down everything you can think of.
2 Now re-read the question and add ✓ ✗ ?
3 Now number all the ticks in the order you think best.

Do any of the **?** bits seem to fit in? Unless you are sure, forget them for now. When you are writing you may see where they fit in.

This is your mini plan. Now you can start!

If it is an essay write:

Introduction

Middle

Conclusion

> **Brief introduction** Say why it is important and the main areas you will cover (refer to your plan!).
>
> **The middle** Write at least one paragraph for each point on your plan. Look at the question at the end of each paragraph. Can you point out how it addressed the question?
>
> **The conclusion** Briefly say what the main points were. Why is this important?

What to do if you go blank

This happens to everyone sometimes. Try these:

- leave a space, it may come back later
- relax – try tensing *all* your muscles and then, starting at the head, relax them one by one
- go back to the title and pick out keywords, scribble notes for anything you can remember about these for 2 minutes.

In extreme circumstances, take a mental break. Think of a time or place when you felt happy. Relive the moment in your head for a minute or two to calm you down. If you 'blank' often, choose this time/place in advance for a quick getaway.

After the exam

Now – forget it. There is no more you can do and worrying will only stress you.

Later on ... before the next exam! Think about what happened. See pp. 112–15 for possible problems and suggestions.

What happened?

Before the exam	During	After	Action
Preparation good	Planning awful	Remembered something I missed out	Practise planning! See p. 118
-	Froze	-	Think about how I can deal with this next time. See p. 119
Your thoughts here …			

Multiple choice questions (MCQs)

MCQs test your dyslexia as much as your subject knowledge. You need to process lots of similar information and recall matching information from your memory, all under timed conditions. This is a bit like a 'spot the difference' competition.

Obviously revising well will help you spot a matching answer quickly (once you have processed the question), making your response as automatic as possible.

After reading the question, **try to recall the answer before running through the options**. This reduces the amount of processing you do and makes the right answer easier to spot.

GUESS any questions you don't know; even if the exam is negatively marked this should pay off. If there are 4 possible answers and you can eliminate one and another looks unlikely, then you have a 50% chance of being correct – and that is a pass.

Dealing with seminars, group work and presentations

Seminars: useful – and challenging!

Dyslexic students can really shine in seminars, especially if they have a verbal/listening learning style. Seminars can be very constructive as they revisit the lecture, usually applying it to a real-life situation. Practising, discussing or doing a presentation on a scenario makes the purpose of what you are learning clearer.

Excellent though seminars can be, they can present issues for dyslexic students:

- Seminars held shortly after the lecture do not allow time to review any lecture material before you have to apply this knowledge.
- Even when you know the answer to a question, it takes time to recall the answer or consider how to make a point. By the time you are ready the moment has passed.
- Making presentations is often a dyslexic strength – but it needs good organisational (and sequencing) skills.

> When answering questions or making a point, keep sentences short and don't be tempted to over-explain.

TOP TIP — If you can, pick a seminar time furthest from the lecture time to give you time to review any notes or do some pre-reading (use the Start and End method, see pp. 58–62).

Group work: making it work for you

Many dyslexic students really enjoy group work. It works well with their dyslexic and individual working style. It allows them to shine at some aspects such as speaking and discussion without the need to read and write.

If you are a good talker other students may just assume you are good at everything else. So be aware there are some pitfalls of group work for dyslexic students.

Beware!	Why? Because ...	Try this instead
Volunteering to do writing	You may be better at other stuff!	Making visual aids, presenting, advising?
Being unrealistic	It is hard to know how much you can do in a short time.	'Buddy up' to share tasks; take on less than you think you can manage!

Beware!	Why? Because …	Try this instead
Organisation issues	Times, dates and meetings are not your strong point.	Note times/dates carefully. Make sure you have a reminder (email, text, alarm).
Over-stimulation	If many ideas are suggested you may get distracted or confused.	Better to focus on one or two ideas only. Leave the rest to someone else.

Most of all, enjoy it!

Keep a record of meetings

An up-to-date version of this can be found at: www.brookes.ac.uk/services/upgrade/pdf/groupwork.pdf

Presentations

'Winging it' can be disastrous … as your dodgy short-term memory means you may:

▶ lose your place in the presentation
▶ get distracted and go off on a tangent
▶ skip bits you meant to include

Groupwork Record of meetings

Meeting no ____ Date / time _____ Place _____

Group's research topic area
_____

Who present
_____
_____
_____

Outcomes of discussion
•
•
•

Actions

WHAT needs doing?	WHO will do it?	HOW? Detail	By WHEN?

Date and time of next meeting
_____

- find it difficult to sequence your stuff
- find managing time problematic.

Even when you know your material well you need to do some planning to reduce the effect of your dyslexia – which is always worse when you are under pressure.

So, PLAN!

Plan:

- how you will keep on track
- what you will use to time it
- how you will start and end
- how you will deal with questions.

Keeping on track

It doesn't matter what you use, but do use something – don't leave it to chance.

Cards

TOP TIP Do NOT use lengthy notes – you may just end up reading them out …

Managing time

▶ Avoid fiddling with your phone; set your timer going (check it is on silent).
▶ Write the finish time on top of your presentation notes/cards.
▶ Ask a friend to signal when you have just a few minutes left.
▶ Identify a chunk of material you can skim over (or miss out) if time is tight.

Managing questions

Dealing with questions is best left to the end if you can, or you may go off track.

Do	Why (and what to do if it goes wrong)
Repeat the question	To check you got it and so the audience knows what was asked.
Answer the question	If you don't know, say 'What an interesting point; does anyone know the answer to that?'. If no one does (that will make you feel better!), say you will find out and ask the questioner to leave their details afterwards so you can get back to them (and do!!!).
Ask the questioner if that answered their question	To check if they are happy! If not, ask to them to explain and start the process again.

12 A final word ... have confidence to study your own way!

The message from this book has been to think about how you learn best (metacognition) in order to improve your effectiveness. The strategies outlined can help, but have the confidence to develop strategies of your own. Use the LITTLE and OFTEN dyslexic learning style and do it *your* way.

Accepting support

It will not say that you are dyslexic on your qualification certificate. The extra support available at university/college is there to allow you to reach your full potential, so do not hesitate to take it up – it is your entitlement. Try not to leave this until you sit down to write your dissertation!

Be an ambassador for dyslexia – and teach your tutors how to teach you!

Ask for notes to be put on the VLE before lectures; explain that it helps you deal with the lecture content if you can preview notes. Ask if you can record what is said at dissertation supervision meetings or ask them to make notes for you – explain that it is not possible for you to listen and note take simultaneously due to memory and processing difficulties. They want to learn how best to support you, so it is up to you to (gently) guide them. Other dyslexic students will benefit from this too.

PART 3

SUPPORT FOR DYSLEXIC STUDENTS AT UNIVERSITY

Support at university

There is excellent support at university for dyslexic students. If you have funding from the DSA (Disabled Students' Allowance) you will not have to pay for this.

This could provide access to:

- one-to-one study skills support
- computer with assistive software, printer, scanner, maybe a digital recorder
- training to use the assistive software
- an allowance for consumables such as paper, books, photocopying.

You can find out information about the DSA in higher education from a Student Finance England publication called 'Bridging the Gap' (available online) or from www.yourdsa.com/

Finding out what is available at your institution

Every university has a dyslexia/SpLD (Specific Learning Difference) disability support team, usually within Student Services. Universities vary in the way they organise support, so investigate what is available at your institution.

International (and some other) students may not be eligible for DSA to fund their support. But your university may provide help you can access, so do ask!

I think I may be dyslexic – what next?

Dyslexia does not just happen. If you are dyslexic you will always have been dyslexic. It is worth investigating now.

There are free adult screeners or checklists available online such as the one from the Adult Dyslexia Organisation: www.adult-dyslexia.org/info.html. This has 12 questions to determine the chance of being dyslexic.

If this indicates dyslexia is a possibility, contact your university's dyslexia/SpLD team. They can arrange for you to see a specialist to talk it over with. If they agree that dyslexia is a possibility, they will recommend you have a full dyslexia/SpLD assessment and tell you how to arrange this.

Why is an assessment needed?

A full diagnostic assessment is key to getting support for any SpLD or disability at university. This has to comply with guidelines and is required before you can apply for any funding, such as DSA.

You cannot register at your university as a student requiring any kind of specialist support without this evidence.

If I have had exam arrangements before, can I have them at uni?

Maybe! But if you had a short version of an assessment (usually called 'access arrangements') to allow extra time in exams or some extra support at college or school this **MAY NOT be enough evidence** to register for support and apply for DSA at university.

Check with your university's SpLD advisers. They will advise if you need to go for a full assessment and tell you how to do this.

What happens at the assessment?

A full diagnostic assessment will take at least 2 hours and the final report may be many pages. It needs to test for the main characteristics of dyslexia – difficulties with short-term memory, working memory and processing speed.

Some of the tests are quite fun and many students enjoy the activities, but of course there will be some tests you find difficult if you are dyslexic. You cannot pass a dyslexia assessment without revealing some underlying problems with memory and processing!

The assessor will ask some questions about your background and educational experience. The tests consider cognitive abilities, strengths and difficulties and come to a conclusion about any SpLD you may have. If a SpLD is found, the report will recommend what support would be useful to help with this.

Be sure to access any help available

Your degree or Masters certificate won't say you are dyslexic or if you accessed any available support. Students who take up one-to-one study support and/or use assistive technology often comment that they don't know what they would have done without it.

Living and studying at university is very demanding and this extra stress can make dyslexia more apparent. Many dyslexic students manage well until crunch points such as their dissertation or exams. Make sure you know what is available and how to arrange support *before* you hit these moments, so you are prepared.

One-to-one study skills support

Universities vary in how they provide one-to-one support. Some organise this for you and you attend sessions within the university; others may put you in touch with a tutor and you arrange times and where to meet.

How to get the most out of one-to-one sessions

One-to-one support sessions for dyslexic students at university cover many of the skills outlined in this book. The advantage for you is that these will be tailored to your particular requirements.

It may be useful for the tutor to see a copy of your diagnostic assessment report at your first meeting and answer any questions you have about it. The tutor will of course discuss your strengths and limitations and suggest strategies to cope with these.

It is useful if you come prepared for sessions with any course handbooks (or know how to access them on the VLE). If you have any particular concerns that you want addressed, do speak up! Sometimes it can be daunting speaking about your difficulties but your tutor is there to support you through it and it should be a positive experience. You can always change tutor later if you need to.

References

Buzan T (2003) *Use your head*. London: BBC, p64.

Cottrell S (2008). *The study skills handbook*, 3rd edition. Basingstoke: Palgrave Macmillan.

Middlebrook RD (1990). *The textmapping project.* Available at: www.textmapping.org/ [Accessed 16 October 2011].

Rose J (2009). *Identifying and teaching children and young people with dyslexia and literacy difficulties*. An independent report from Sir Jim Rose to the Secretary of State for Children, Schools and Families. Available at: https://www.education.gov.uk/publications/eOrderingDownload/00659-2009DOM-EN.pdf

Torgesen JK (1981). The study of short-term memory in learning disabled children: goals, methods and conclusions. In Gadow K and Bialer I (eds), *Advances in learning and behavioural disabilities*, vol. 1 (pp117–50). Greenwich, CT: JAI Press.

Westminster School (no date). The forgetting curve. Available at: www.rgsinfo.net/subject/learning%20support/pdfs/TheForgettingCurve(Westminster).pdf [Accessed 7 January 2012].

Williams K (1995). *Writing essays*. Oxford: Oxford Centre for Staff Development.

Useful contacts

Being Dyslexic: www.beingdyslexic.co.uk/

British Dyslexia Association: www.bdadyslexia.org.uk/

DfES: www.direct.gov.uk/en/DisabledPeople/EducationAndTraining/HigherEducation/DG_10034898

Dyslexia Action: www.dyslexiaaction.org.uk/

Dyslexia Scotland: www.dyslexiascotland.org.uk

Helen Arkell Discovery Centre: www.arkellcentre.org.uk/

National Network of Assessment Centres: www.nnac.org/

yourDSA: www.yourdsa.com

Useful resources

BrainHE: www.brainhe.com/index.html

Hull University – *Bumper guide to writing*: www2.hull.ac.uk/Student/pdf/dyswritebumper.pdf

Hull University – Mind maps for everything.

Hull University – Reading skills SQ3R mind map.

Leicester University online study guides: www2.le.ac.uk/offices/ssds/accessability/study-skills/study-guides

MyStudyBar: http://eduapps.org/?page_id=7

Sheffield University – Study skills for students with dyslexia: http://dyslexstudyskills.group.shef.ac.uk/

VARK: www.vark-learn.com/

YouTube: www.youtube.com/ and http://utubersity.com/ for visual virtual lessons and podcasts

Index

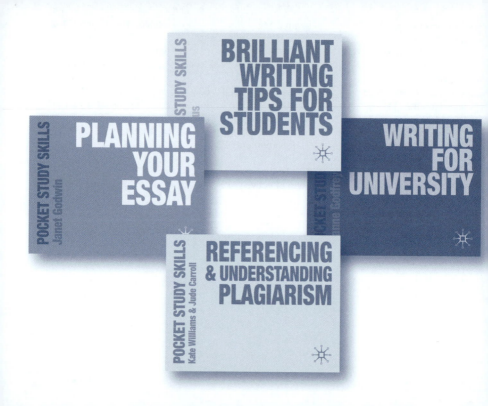

POCKET STUDY SKILLS
STUDY SKILLS

BRILLIANT
WRITING
TIPS FOR
STUDENTS

PLANNING
YOUR
ESSAY
Janet Godwin

WRITING
FOR
UNIVERSITY

POCKET STUDY SKILLS
Kate Williams & Jude Carroll

REFERENCING
& UNDERSTANDING
PLAGIARISM

POCKET STUDY SKILLS
STUDY SKILLS
DOING RESEARCH
nas

POCKET STUDY SKILLS
Lucinda Becker
14 DAYS TO EXAM SUCCESS

POCKET STUD
anne Godfrey
READING AND MAKING NOTES

POCKET STUDY SKILLS
Peter Hartley & Mark Bawson
SUCCESS IN GROUPWORK